HEALING
ON THE OTHER SIDE

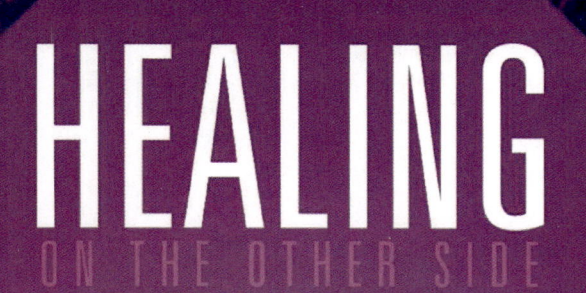

BY CHARLENE EVANS

Healing On The Other Side
Copyright © 2019 by Charlene Evans

ISBN: 978-1-7330534-0-2
Published by Chiccy Baritone Unlimited, LLC
Atlanta, Georgia

Edited by: Andrea C. Jasmin / A.C. Jasmin Proofreading
Cover Design by: Mia Salley / Designs By Mia
Interior Design by: Tammy Carpenter / Effectual Concepts
About the Author Photograph: Hope Ballenger Photography
Back Cover Photograph: Drea Nicole Photography

All rights reserved. This book or any portion thereof may not be reproduced or used in any manner whatsoever without the express written permission of the publisher except for the use of brief quotations in a book review.

Printed in the United States of America

DEDICATION

*This book is dedicated to my mom, **Viola C. Evans**.*
A wife, mother, grandmother, co-worker, sister, auntie, and friend.

I Love You Forever.

FOREWORD

"Go play outside! But, be back in here before the street lights come on." "If Mary jumped off the bridge, are you going to jump off too?" "Eat everything on your plate. They're starving children in Africa!" "Don't let anybody have to tell me they saw you somewhere acting up!"

Well . . . there is a strong possibility you would probably only understand these phrases if you had an "old-school" mother. You know what I mean by "old-school" right? Well, let me be a little more specific, just in case.

An "old-school" mother was . . .

The mother who held, deeply in her heart, the messages she gleaned from the village that nurtured her and now she was passing along the same messages. You know, she was the mother who believed it was her role to instill morals, integrity, wisdom, and values into those she brought into this world. It was this mother who wrapped her heart around her family with the tapestry of pieces she collected from her own life's journey. This mother was the one who wore motherhood like a badge of honor. Because for her, there was no greater honor bestowed.

I am certainly not suggesting that today's mothers don't have these same tendencies, I am simply setting the stage for who you will meet in the pages that follow.

Allow me to give you a bit of preparation for what you will encounter.

You are about to step onto the evolutionary paths of a mother and daughter. You will quickly see that this is no ordinary pair. In fact, you're going to have to remind yourself that you have not snuggled with the next great fiction novel in your hands. Instead, you'll need to remember that this is a very real storyline of laughter, lessons, longsuffering, limitations, longing, letting go, and love.

This book was not written based upon theoretical frameworks for parenting. The book is not based upon research findings from scholars who have studied family dynamics and behavior.

This book was written through the eyes of a child who has learned womanhood from the woman who modeled it for her. Now, as the narrator of this remarkable account, she has granted us all access into her sacred space.

As you carefully and prayerfully engage, it is my hope you will make yourself at home with this mother and daughter. After all, isn't that where the heart is? So, come on in; you're welcome here.

Dr. Katrina Hutchins (Dr. K)
Entrepreneur, Author, Speaker, Personal & Executive Coach
Re-Source Solutions

CONTENTS

Introduction vii

Chapter 1: November 24, 2009 1

Chapter 2: November 25, 2009 9

Chapter 3: December 10, 2009 15

Chapter 4: April 15, 2010 23

Chapter 5: April 29, 2010 31

Chapter 6: May 6, 2010 39

Chapter 7: May 19, 2010 45

Chapter 8: May 25, 2010 51

Chapter 9: May 26, 2010 59

Chapter 10: June 7, 2010 67

Chapter 11: June 23, 2010 73

Chapter 12: July 13, 2010 79

Chapter 13: July 28, 2010 87

Chapter 14: August 17, 2010 93

Chapter 15: April 2, 2011 99
My Housewarming

Chapter 16: April 26, 2011 105
New Beginnings

About The Author...115

INTRODUCTION

My mom, Viola C. Evans, was born on Feb 11, 1952 in Hopkins, SC, located on the outskirts of Columbia, SC to the parents of Rufus and Viola Wilson. She is one of 9 children who attended Hopkins Elementary School, which included first grade all the way to eighth grade then Hopkins High which is now called Lower Richland High School where she was a cheerleader. She furthered her education at Benedict College where she graduated with a Bachelor's Degree in Business Administration. Throughout her life she always found a way to be involved in sports, such as softball, and was known to be a great athlete overall. Momma was also a great cook and often chosen to do the cooking for her mother and grandmother. She married Joseph L. Evans on June 22, 1972, had 3 children, Quanita, Charlene, and DeWayne, and absolutely loved being a wife and mother.

But along the journey of life Viola experienced a health scare that shook everyone...

November 22, 2009 will be a day I will never forget.

Things were changing rapidly with my mom's health and communication—not only with medical staff, but also with family was very important. Throughout this time, in order to keep everyone informed on her status, my dad kept a voice recorder in the hospital room and would record updates from doctors and nurses since it was so much information and easy to forget. My sister would send out text messages to family and friends and I would send out emails. These emails later became not only updates but encouragement for me and others as I tried to report my mom's status from my point of view. These updates are now a part of this memoir of a very critical time in my mom's life.

My prayer is that whatever stage you are in with someone who is going through health challenges, that you stay encouraged and remain open to learning on this journey. There will be good times, bad times, sad times, and encouraging times, but no matter what emotion you may be experiencing at any given time, remain in HOPE and LOVE.

CHAPTER 1

Tuesday, November 24, 2009

Healing On The Other Side

"Evans, Charlene"
11/24/2009 09:52 AM

To

cc

Subject: update on my mom

Wanted to give an update on my mom:

Spoke with my sister on yesterday (Monday, Nov 23rd) at 7pm and I have good news! The build up of fluid was discovered from a numerous amount of "Abscess" that were on the lining of her stomach that were not detected on the "Cat Scan" that they have been doing over the years (approx 3yrs). Also, the electrolytes in her body were high to the point that her once failing kidney (as a result of the fluid) was producing "urine" again. (she has been doing dialysis treatment for about 4 weeks now) so they are testing the urine and checking that out to make sure everything is okay and its filtering out waste properly.

She is still scheduled to undergo colon surgery today at 4:30pm.

I thank you all for your prayers and your concern! I truly give God all the honor and glory for bringing forth revelation to the issue in my mom's body which has been going on for years! And even though she has another surgery to go, I will continue to speak LIFE and HEALING in her body, in the mighty name of Jesus! This is just so awesome and I am so glad she is on her way to full recovery! Please continue to keep my family in prayer!

Love,

Charlene

Healing On The Other Side

Two days. Just two days from a health scare that our family experienced with my mom on Sunday, November 22, 2009. My father's account of what was going on in those moments prior to calling for help sounded pretty scary as he explains that what he observed happening to my mom in the early morning hours looked like "death trying to visit." He called an ambulance and explained that even when they arrived, they were "working on my mom" before pulling off. To hear this story from my father while we were in the waiting area at the hospital shook me to my core. I can't imagine being in his shoes and having to make a quick decision in such a critical moment. Surrounded by family, we were all waiting to hear what the doctor was going to say. As my father was getting updates on my mom's condition after being admitted to the Intensive Care Unit, they discovered a hole in my mom's colon and it was leaking waste into her body, poisoning her and slowly shutting down her organs. Over several years my mom developed several health issues so this incident was a crescendo of events that lead to this major scare.

This is my momma. The "glue" that keeps the family together. The comedian and funny woman who will make you laugh just off of her laugh. The light of my life and my personality "twin." We were so much alike that we bumped heads often. However, we agreed on more than we disagreed. I was always pretty vocal about how I feel and known to be a 'talker' even though it took me longer than the average child to even start talking. I can remember my mom telling me the story about me being around two years old and not really talking. It was a concern of hers so she took me to the doctor and he assured her that nothing was wrong with me. I'll start talking when I'm ready. Then she concludes the story by saying, "And once you started talking, we have not been able to shut you up since!" That makes me laugh when I think about that story because my mom could never tell it without laughing at the end. But here I am . . . looking at my mom in ICU with a tube down her throat unable to speak. Speechless . . . but thinking to myself, "I would love to get into a verbal exchange with you right now." To hear her voice would have meant the world to me because we spoke just about every day, even after I graduated from college and moved to Greenville, SC. The induced coma that she was in, according to the doctors, allowed healing to take place in her body. I'm looking at the family Matriarch who was our main flow of love and communication. Her role was crucial in so many ways but her ability to communicate her children whereabouts to my dad was like an "air traffic control center." All information channeled through my mom and she would communicate our "locations" and anything going on with us back to daddy. She was so dope like that. I would watch her while in her presence as she made multiple lists and took pride into being a wife and mother.

But just like that . . . she was in the ICU. Unable to speak and waiting to go into surgery. Life can change in a blink of an eye. Unaware of the timeline of this journey, my sister and I decided to create multiple ways to communicate my mom's status in the hospital to family and friends and asked that they help us get the word out. My sister would send out a mass text message and I would draft emails and only send when there were milestone updates. A lot of times that included several days of events explaining what was happening concerning her health and progress. This made it so much easier on us; cutting down on the amount of times we had to duplicate her status to every person that asked. After her surgery I knew there would be a recovery period and shortly after I figured she would be coming home soon because the issue would be fixed, right? Wrong . . . this ended up being the beginning of a journey with her health and a walk with God that challenged my faith in insurmountable ways. A journey that I will never forget for as long as I am living. As a result of this journey, my life will never be the same. I had to live out my belief in God and His word according to what it means for healing to occur on the "other side." I faced the fear of her presence not making it past this moment and I would cut off the thought prematurely because surely she will make it through this? Right God?

CHAPTER

2

Wednesday, November 25, 2009

From: Evans, Charlene
Sent: Wednesday, November 25, 2009 9:08 AM
Subject: Update on Mom - Tuesday, Nov 24th

Just wanted to give an update on my mom as of yesterday! She is progressing along very well. Her doctor could not find the initial issue with the Colon so he decided to not do the surgery and allow her body to heal due to the swelling from the first surgery and to also not put anymore stress on her body. She is still in ICU, heavily sedated, but responding when you touch her hand, her hair or her face...she is resting and looking very peaceful! (according to my father and sister) I thought to myself when I heard how good she looked resting that only God can grant us the "Perfect Peace" that we need...She will be in the hospital for another week while they monitor her body and her breathing and maybe even longer depending on how she is progressing the next couple of week!

I can't thank everyone who has prayed for me and my family enough! Your fervent prayers and confessions have been a blessing! The almighty hears you and receives you so once again I say, Thank You! Have a very blessed and Thankful time with your family and friends throughout this Holiday Season...first stop, Thanksgiving! (smile)

Much Love,

Charlene

At the time everything was transpiring with my mom, she was in Columbia, SC and I was living in Greenville, SC. My sister was keeping me updated on mom's status while I was trying to finish out the half work week to head home for Thanksgiving, which was Thursday, November 26, 2009. There was no question where I would be spending the holiday and as much as I disliked being in the hospital, the most important person in my life was there: my mom. Being there with her was my main priority as I juggled working and living one and a half hours away. My weekends for the next nine months were dedicated to putting in my weekend "shift" with momma. My father, my sister, and I would rotate our time making sure someone was there around the clock. I honestly didn't know how long my mom was going to be in the hospital but my thoughts were however long it takes, Lord, heal her body. Take away the pain that she was feeling. When she comes out of this, her testimony will definitely be a blessing to every heart and ear that hears it. I can't wait to hear her testify and tell it in "Viola's own special way" which of course will include some humor and that laugh that I miss so much. The laugh that I could remember waking up to on a Saturday morning hearing bits and pieces of her conversations to her friends, her sisters, and her nieces. Her jovial spirit and "Viola-isms" are contagious! Everyone that was around my mom long enough would pick up on some of her "Viola-isms" like:

(phone ringing)

(momma picks up): "Hello? It's your dime—speak!" (When payphones were a dime to use)

or

(*phone ringing*)

(momma picks up): "House of beauty, this is cutie!"

Standing or sitting by her bedside was a hard reality and surreal. To be looking over a woman who has spent her life looking over you. To be on the outside of the bed when I'm use to her being on the outside of the bed taking care of me. To be positioned in a way that felt helpless, but not Godless, gave me the hope I needed to see my mom come through whole and complete . . . nothing missing and nothing broken. My visual of this moment in time began to prepare my faith for the only outcome I was willing to accept at the time and that was my mom walking out of this hospital. Period. *So God, as the family and myself pray, I trust you to heal her on this side.*

CHAPTER

3

Thursday, December 10, 2009

Evans, Charlene

From: Evans, Charlene
Sent: Thursday, December 10, 2009 1:59 PM
Subject: update on my mom - Dec 10th

Hello All:

Hope all is well. Just wanted to give an update on my mom. She had surgery scheduled for Monday of this week but it was postponed until further notice because she is now starting to have issues breathing. They put her back on the ventilator and checked her vitals and she appears to be fine but just didn't want to take any chances with her having trouble breathing. She is definitely ready to go home and becoming anxious and tired of laying down with no option to stand up or walk around because she is still "open" and getting the "dressings" on her incision cleaned and monitored daily. She is still in ICU and though restless, she is doing okay. I can't imagine what she is going through but I am continuing to pray for her to stay focused on regaining her strength and healing! God has brought her a "mighty" long way and even though there is a long road of recovery ahead, she is still progressing despite her breathing and I trust GOD. Period. (smile)

Thank you all for your prayers and concerns and please, keep her on your prayer list!

Blessings,

Charlene

It's been over two weeks and momma is still in the ICU. My first thought was, "I didn't think that she would still be there." Yes, she has gone through some serious health challenges, but really God? And now surgery has been postponed due to her having trouble breathing. There were times I would look at her when she was not looking at me. Wondering how she was processing all of this. How was she "really" feeling? What was going on in her mind? Did she question God? Even though she is conscious now, at one point in the ICU she was not conscious. So during that time, was she having a nonverbal conversation with Jesus? Was she scared to die? Was she feeling like she was not going to fully recover? So many questions but my momma was not going to tell me anything that she felt would have me worried. I would dare to say that no mother wants their child to worry about them. Instead they prefer to do all of the worrying for them. My mom was in a vulnerable state that compromised her ability to be momma the way that she wanted to be momma. But guess what? I believe my mom felt the same way I felt every time I would come in that room but she never would ask and I'm sure she had her reasons. She would always smile and make small talk but I believe my mom was probably wondering how was I really doing? Was I scared and thinking she was going to die when she was rushed to the hospital? Do I feel like she's not going to recover from this? These were questions that she never asked and conversations that I never had with her. While in the moment, my thoughts and prayers were on the fact that she was still alive and although progress was happening slowly, it was still happening and that was all that mattered to me.

Uncertainty is very hard to comprehend or communicate. Trust with no guarantee is hard to maintain especially when what you see contradicts what you believe. My Christian journey intersecting this moment with momma didn't turn me away from God but rather brought me closer because in my understanding and knowledge, He is the only one who is not surprised or caught off guard from this situation. This is a part of His plan for my mom's life as we watched, looked, listened, prayed, and learned more about God in all of His might. His thoughts are not our thoughts and His ways are not our ways, but in order for me to gain insight on what was happening I had to seek Him in a way I never have before and put my feelings, and thoughts at times, aside in order to be present with Him and represent Him while I experience this traumatic event. My desire to know God was never limited to prayer, quoting scripture, attending church or Christian conferences, listening to gospel music only, or proclaiming the gospel without a real relationship with Him that would oftentimes would be tested. Everything God invested in me at this point in my life was about to be applied because everything we go through is not by accident or unnecessary battles. God is intentional and His Purpose for our lives will include trials.

"²Consider it pure joy, my brothers and sisters, whenever you face trials of many kinds, ³because you know that the testing of your faith produces perseverance. ⁴Let perseverance finish its work so that you may be mature and complete, not lacking anything." - James 1:2-4 (NIV)

What I have witnessed in this short amount of time has already given me a profound appreciation for understanding perseverance.

> **PERSERVERANCE**: continued effort to do or achieve something despite difficulties, failure, or opposition: the action or condition or an instance of persevering: STEADFASTNESS (www.merriam-webster.com)

Maintaining a positive attitude and speaking LIFE for momma every time I walked in that hospital room, despite what I was about to walk into, was very difficult at times. However, I know it was building my **perseverance**, **faith** and **hope** ultimately leading to her coming out of this situation healed and better than she was when it all happened.

God, help me to represent PERSEVERANCE for my momma in those days where she can't find the strength or courage.

God, help me to represent PERSEVERANCE for my family in those days where they can't find the strength

God, when I have moments when I don't feel like PERSEVERING, put someone in my presence that could represent PERSEVERANCE for me.

CHAPTER 4

Thursday, April 15, 2010

Healing On The Other Side

From: Evans, Charlene
Sent: Thursday, April 15, 2010 1:47 PM
Subject: update on my mom 4-15-10

Hello All:

Just want to update you on my mom. She was released from the hospital on Monday, March 29th and admitted to a rehabilitation facility for speech and physical therapy. She has not spent a full week there yet because of complications with her heart and blood pressure in which the facility, not being a hospital, didn't want to take any chances so they admitted her to the hospital. She was at the hospital from Thursday, April 1st to Monday, April 5th then sent back to rehabilitation center because she was doing better.

Today, a few minutes ago, I just received information from my sister that her blood pressure dropped tremendously putting her at risk for a stroke, heart attack or brain damage. She has been admitted back to the hospital, in ICU and currently stable.

What a warrior, a fighter. I was there with her the past two weekends at the hospital and we had such a good time with each other. She is truly fighting for her life and I once again ask to keep her lifted in prayer! She has come a loooong way and I'm not giving up on her. I believe that God can heal her and until his work in her is done, she is here and needing the prayers of the saints.

Thanks,

Charlene

I can't imagine what was going on in her mind. I believe that when you are battling sickness in your body, you are at the mercy of God and vulnerable. I know my mom didn't always communicate a lot of her truth and those moments when she felt horrible. She really didn't want to be looked upon as "whoa is me." In my mind she was a "super woman" without trying to be and never advertised herself that way. There was no cap, boots, or even a tight suit but she always found a way to save the day. She was creative and thoughtful and knew how to do so much with so little. I have countless stories that can never fill enough pages in a book but I can remember a time in college where I called my mom in the early morning hours complaining that I was having a "heart attack" and she laughed at first then said, "Charlene, if you were, you would be speaking to me much different then you are right now so what's going on?" I told her about the pain in my chest. Then she asked, "What did you eat tonight while studying?" And I told her about the wings and fries I brought from "The Pit" on campus and some other things I was snacking on while agonizing over a test I had in a few days. She then began to question my inventory of medicine and when she didn't hear anything that she felt could help she said, "go get a cup of water, warm it up in the microwave until it is very hot, not boiling, and sip it slow because it sounds like you have GAS."

GAS momma?!?!?! Really? I thought it was ridiculous but OK...

So I did what she said and tried to lay back down with the hopes of getting some sleep since I knew I had class in the morning. A few hours later, the pain went away in my chest but now I had War World III under my covers! Momma was right! It was GAS!

We laughed about it the next day as I called her back excited for my relief and amazed at how she knew what to do whether I felt like I was dying or hungry. It didn't stop with health and wellness but also with my stomach. Momma showed me how to perform miracles in the kitchen. Although I didn't have to feed 5,000 people with five barley loaves and two small fish, I felt like I could if I needed to. She taught me how to stretch $10 into enough meals that would last me three days, eating twice a day. It's called, "Crockpot recipes."

God, I wish I was able to give her a remedy or miracle right now.

My mom was fighting for her life and it was very difficult to see her go through so much in her body. The back and forth between progression and regression had to be very frustrating. I do believe that whatever is going on in the mind affects what is going on in the body. I wonder what she was thinking at that time and what was going on in her mind that affected what was going on in her body and the result that had on her healing process. Because if nothing more, my mom loves her kids and her grandbaby and her will to live for herself and her family was evident. I can remember when we would go visit her in the hospital she would have all of these pictures hanging up of Nymah, her only grandbaby at the time, and we would ask in a "fake jealous kind of way," "Where are OUR pictures Momma?" (Laughing) because she loved that grandbaby. I couldn't imagine my mom not wanting nothing more than to live for and see her children and grandbaby prosper, but also fighting for her health. In my heart, I really wish she would have communicated more but my mind understands to a certain extent as to why she chose not to. However, I also believe that the blessing was in her not communicating the vulnerabilities that she experienced with us but instead kept it between her and God. When someone is sick and in a hospital connected to so many tubes and monitors and you have no control over what's going on, it challenges every emotion and every decision you make. You will never fully know how they feel unless you are in their shoes, so my perception and my thought process was very limited based on what my mom did not communicate and what was actually going on in her. I really applaud her strength. There are times when courage is loud and there are times when courage is quiet. For me, I held on to this new approach to courage like a toddler to a mom's leg in a room full of strangers. I loved it and never wanted to let go. My momma taught me how to be strong in the midst of her storm.

CHAPTER

5

Thursday,
April 29, 2010

From: Evans, Charlene
Sent: Thursday, April 29, 2010 9:08 AM
Subject: update on my mom 4-29-10

Good Morning,

Just wanted to update you on my mom. She was released back to the rehabilitation center on Monday April 26th then last night, Wed, April 28th I received a text from my sister which was followed up with a phone call to her and my father. My mom was rushed to the emergency room because her blood sugar was in the 300's, her heart rate was elevated and she kept vomiting. She is now in the hospital in ICU until further notice. I am going to make my way down to be by her side this afternoon. I was "under the weather" last weekend and could not go down because I did not want her to catch the cold I had.

I am trusting and believing that all things are possible...we can never put a time or demand on what God is doing in our love ones or in the earth but to PRAY..it's the most powerful tool we have and is more than enough. I am encouraged and know that she is in the best care possible right night between the care of the hospital and the care of our awesome God. Much love to you all and I thank you for keeping me encouraged on this journey in my life and the life of my family.

Peace & Blessings,

Charlene

Above 300 . . . yes, my mom's blood sugar was above 300 and because she was diabetic, this was a very dangerous zone measurement in addition to her vomiting continuously. There are so many complications that high blood sugar can cause: problems with your eyes, increased risk of heart disease and stroke, poor wound healing, which could lead to an amputation or decreased kidney function which could eventually lead to dialysis. The vomiting episodes were one of the symptoms of kidney failure. I can remember momma starting dialysis and whether it was a result of this episode or not, it became a part of her life. The nurse gave me permission to sit in on one of my mom's dialysis treatments. It was HARD for me to watch. Looking at her blood being drawn out then sent to the dialyzer where it worked as an external "kidney" filtering out salt, waste, and fluid then the clean blood being sent back into her body. It's a very long process and could last from three to five hours. Watching my mom sit there had my mind all over the place and that would be the last time I would sit in one of her sessions. I remember after mom's dialysis sessions, she would be so tired. I would purposely wait about two hours after every session to give her a call, allowing her time to rest.

Momma was not talking as much due to the trachea that she now had. The main function of a trachea is to provide airflow to and from the lungs for respiration.

While being in the ICU she was relying on a ventilator, which was attached to a tube and placed in momma's airway to help her breathe. After coming out of the ICU she had a temporary tracheostomy and was not able to talk or eat. She was being feed from a tube and because she was having difficulty swallowing I can recall her lips being so dry and her tube having to get cleaned daily. It looked painful when the nurse was cleaning her tube. Periodically throughout the day, the nurse will swab momma's mouth with this sponge tip stick to moisten momma's lips but my momma would also take that time to suck the sponge filled with water. Her dependency felt childlike but her determination was in her eyes. I could feel the warrior in her when I would look at her and smile and she would smile back. Some days she didn't smile but I still felt her smile in her eyes.

My prayer life took another turn in this moment.

When you feel like options are few in what you can do, it's time to PRAY. My engineering mind wanted to find another way because hey, I was taught to look at all perspectives of a problem and create a solution. It worked in the marketplace but this approach didn't work so well right now. This situation was beyond a degree or a few years of work history, but this was one of those moments where my prayer was my tool and God wanted me to consult Him and not myself. He wanted me to surrender and trust Him because between the care of the hospital staff who loved my mom and our Lord, she was in the best care possible. I rerouted my burden (1 Peter 5:7) to him because that's what he told me to do even though I was not always obedient about doing it. God doesn't need my help, but would someone please remind me every time I try to assist Him? I feel like God looks at me the same way my mom would look at me in those times when she would be in the kitchen cooking and I would try to solicit my help. Most times she never had to say a word but just look and I got the message. In this moment right now I didn't need to be told to get out of the way because God definitely was making moves that I could both see and not see.

CHAPTER

6

Thursday, May 6, 2010

From: Evans, Charlene
Sent: Thursday, May 06, 2010 1:06 PM
Subject: update on my mom 5-6-10

Hello All:

Just wanted to give you an update on my mom. The last update on 4-29-10 stated how she was rushed back to the hospital because of her sugar level being in the 300s, vomiting and irregular heart. Well she has been put in a regular room and out of ICU since Sunday, May 2nd which is all great news! She had her "third" swallow test, the first two were unsuccessful but like they say, three time's a CHARM, she past this third test and had her first "solid" meal on Wednesday (May 5th) since not having any solid food since Nov 22, 2009. Praise God!! Her meal was: Mash potatoes, carrots, hamburger pattie and angel food cake...Yah Momma!!! (smile)

Her stay at the hospital right now is indefinite but this is major progress eating solid foods again. I am so excited and can't wait to see her on Sunday. Thank you all for your continuous prayers! You will probably never know what that means to me and my family however, I will continue to remind you!

Be blessed......Happy Early Mother's Day....I think it almost goes without saying, "Cherish your MOTHER'S...you only have ONE and even if the relationship is not perfect, she is YOURS!" (SMILE)

Much Love,

Charlene

Momma is now back eating solid foods after having two unsuccessful swallow test. I'm the daughter of a fighter and there was never an obstacle that my mom was not willing to overcome no matter what. I'm reminded of a line in a pledge that I took when I was younger, in a girls etiquette club, called the "Culturettes." The line said, "Persistent good will break down barriers." When you give your best at the time and it still isn't good enough, you keep on trying until that goal is reached. This was one of many goals that my momma has yet to accomplish and I was confident that one day she would be walking out of the hospital. To think that almost six months ago my family and I experienced one of the greatest health scares with my mom and she is still here. It could have been a much different outcome but she has been fighting ever since and I made sure she would not be in this fight alone. I had groups of people at my church, my job, and friends praying for my mom and keeping me encouraged. I always appreciated when someone would ask me about momma and how she was doing even if at the time we had a minor or major setback. There was no setback that was going to overshadow the fact that she was still alive. Going into the Mother's Day holiday with my mom still here meant everything to me and took on a different meaning after witnessing everything she had endured. Being a poet and my mom being my biggest fan, I decided to write her a poem and frame it for her hospital room:

Poem for my mom on Mother's Day

I hold the hands of the woman who is responsible for carrying out the plan of God for my existence in the earth **My Mother**

The same hands that have embrace me as an infant and an adult in times of triumphant and trouble letting me know you are present because your touch is distinct from any other woman

These hands I hold have been through some hard times, some of the stories I may never know but I feel the "texture" of VICTORY and the spirit of RESILIENCE

As your body and mind persevere through all of the changes taking place

I can only imagine what is going on "inside" of you

Because at one time I was there inside of you, connected to you physically with an umbilical cord that was responsible for feeding me and keeping me alive as you endured the changes of your body and your mind in preparation of my arrival

And even though that umbilical cord was cut and I am no longer attached physically,

I am spiritually attached to you always even when I am not physically here

Feeling the residue of what you may be going through

Day in and out as my spirit intercedes for your needs

So hold my hand and let me be your strength

Giving you what you have given me
RESILIENCE *and* **VICTORY**

Remember soldier, the battle is not yours, it's the LORD's so keep God lifted with worship and praise on your lips and don't forget to lift up these **Beautiful Hands!**

I LOVE YOU … Happy Mother's Day … 2010

CHAPTER

7

Wednesday,
May 19, 2010

Evans, Charlene

From: Evans, Charlene
Sent: Wednesday, May 19, 2010 10:59 AM
Subject: update on my mom 5-18-10

Hello All:

Just wanted to give you an update on my mom. Mother's day was wonderful and as always, she was doing well and in good spirits. All week, there were little changes here and there but nothing significant until Sunday, May 16th. That night around 9:30pm her heart rate dropped to 26 and her blood pressure elevated so they had to move her to ICU for treatment. Besides from being very frustrated, if you can only imagine, she is doing better and stable. Monday, May 17th my father and sister met with the doctor to discuss her possibly getting a defibrillator installed due to the irregularity of her heart. There are serious risk associated to having this device if you are a dialysis patient due to infection growing around the device, which can be treated, is a possible occurrence. However, without the device, the increase/decrease heart rate reoccurring without timely treatment could be fatal. Please I ask, for your continuous prayers concerning this matter and for the holy spirit to guide the doctor's and the family into the right decision for my mom. Her body has been through a lot and I know she is growing weary and tire of being in the hospital and from the constant changes in her body.

What a journey this has been but God is in control and the power of prayer is my virtue! I thank you all for being the thread of strength in my life. Continue to keep my mom and my family in prayer!

Much love,

Charlene

Mother's Day was Sunday, May 9, 2010 and I decided to write momma a poem. In an earlier visit to the hospital, I brought my camera and wanted to take pictures of my mom's hands. For me, it's something about the human hands. They tell the story of age and life. Holding my mom's hands and seeing how much they had changed revealed the multiple changes in her health. The dialysis darkened my mom's complexion and I noticed it first in her hands. The physical changes in her hands didn't matter because when I held her hands it was familiar and I could feel the love in her grip. I remember taking the poem up to the hospital and reading it out loud as if I was at a poetry "open mic" to my mom as she smiled from the beginning to the end. She has always been such a fan of my work ever since I discovered the gift of poetry in me while in college. She has watched this gift grow into opportunities that have allowed me to do spoken word on t.v, featured all over the U.S and internationally. I would love to call and read her poems I was working on over the phone or in person because her support meant the world to me. It doesn't matter what age you are, getting confirmation from your mom matters. During the week following Mother's Day momma begin to have some changes happening in her body but nothing significant until the week after Mother's Day that caused her to have to go back to ICU. In my mind I'm saying, "Nooooooooo, not back to the ICU!" How many more times could her body and mind take this? It's a constant thought in the mind, especially for the family of the sick person, to feel and endure everything that is happening. I would say my mom was not the only one in the hospital; WE all were in the hospital. Families go through things like this together, although at times, it feels so fragmented because everyone is processing everything in their own way and most of the time it's not verbalized. As my mom's health continued to go through a myriad of changes, decisions were being discussed with the immediate family and children but the ultimate decision was left up to my father. Making decisions about the health and care of someone has to be scary and intimidating, especially if there are constant changes in how they are responding to certain treatments and procedures. I appreciate my dad being so dedicated to every move that the nurses and doctors made concerning my mom. He would press "record" every time a nurse or doctor would enter the room giving any update so that he could keep up and have enough information in order to make the necessary decisions concerning my mom. If you can only imagine . . . between voice recordings and notes, we all felt like medical students trying to understand and learn more about every diagnosis and procedure. But I do know that my mom seeing at least one of us every day was the best medicine that she could receive. How do I know? That look in her eyes when one of us entered the room. Her family and friends meant everything to her and she meant everything to us. I smile when I think about the stories people would tell me when they would visit mom in the hospital. She would have them in stitches laughing because she didn't want all of the attention on her. Making people laugh came naturally and people loved being around my momma, who a lot of people called Miss Vi.

CHAPTER

8

Wednesday, May 19, 2010

Evans, Charlene

From: Evans, Charlene
Sent: Tuesday, May 25, 2010 8:37 AM
Subject: update on my mom 5-25-10

Hello All:

Just wanted to give you an update on my mom. Spent time with my mom this past weekend both Friday night and Saturday afternoon. She is eating well and looking good☺! At that time she had still not made a decision about the defibrillator until Sunday afternoon. My sister informed me that she decided to have it installed. She is currently being prepped for surgery this morning and it will take place at 9am. The surgery is for 3 hrs so I am asking everyone to take out a moment this morning to lift up Viola Evans to Jesus! That her vitals stay normal as her body undergoes more "cutting" and "work". I pray that the doctors and his staff are alert this morning and knowledgeable in not only the procedure but in keeping everything else that has been considered vital to her health stable (her kidney's, blood sugar, etc.)

Will keep everyone posted on the outcome of the surgery! May God bless you and your family!

Much love,

Charlene

It's always so good seeing my mom during the weekends. This weekend she was enjoying her food and really looking good. These changes in her body were definitely taking a toll on her physically. Knowing that this surgery was coming up, I had so many thoughts going on in my head on my visit as I tried to prepare my heart, mind, and spirit to be in prayer for my mom. The decision was made to proceed with getting the defibrillator installed. An implantable cardioverter-defibrillator or automated implantable cardioverter-defibrillator is a device implantable inside the body, able to perform cardioversion, defibrillation, and pacing of the heart. The device is capable of correcting most life-threatening cardiac arrhythmias. I have since left Columbia, SC and now I'm back in Greenville, SC. It's a normal workday and although I am sitting at my desk, I am mentally absent. Surgery was at 9:00am this morning and all I could do was think about my mom. I really didn't like not being there for her once she woke up from this three-hour procedure, but I knew it would only be a few more days before I would see her and talk about how she was recovering. She's a tough cookie . . . I oftentimes think about my mom and smile . . . she is feisty, and I embody that trait of hers so strongly. This is also the reason why we would "bump heads" which felt like "war," especially in my teenage years. I knew it ALL and there was nothing my mom could tell me.

"God, do you hear me?" Ok, good! Could you make a visit in the operating room and tell my momma that I'm there in spirit? Could you supernaturally take this prayer to her and deliver it straight to her heart while she is unconscious in surgery? I want her to feel every word like a beat keeping her alive because she has to come out of this so that we can have our next argument, hug, kiss and eventually make up like we have done over and over again. Oh, and let her know that there is a tribe of people that are waiting for her because they need her too." Mentally stories begin to flash before my eyes, like that time I got into a really bad car accident driving to Columbia, SC for a candlelight vigil that I was scheduled to do poetry. It was raining really hard and I hydroplaned and landed on the side of the road a few hundred yards from a bridge. I later learned that a UPS driver witnessed the accident while driving behind me and when my car finally came to a stop, he came to my rescue, grabbed my phone, and came across your number to call me. I was pulled out of the car to a crowd of people there for support. Out of nowhere while crying and hugging the UPS driver I looked up and saw you parting the crowd like the red sea making your way straight to me uninhibited, bold and with a look in your eyes I will never forget . . . you grabbed me and held me for what felt like hours. I was so scared and just knew I was dead but God spared my life. You, daddy and Tasha were there for me that night in a way that brings such gratitude to my memory. I was told that when the church learned of my accident they began to pray for me corporately and I'm equally grateful for that. Memories are miracles too because they have the power to instantly transform your mind in moments that can realign your life. As I flash back to now waiting on a phone call from either my sister or my dad on the outcome of your surgery, I'm reminded of God's grace and mercy. He created my mom and he has the final say on her life. He carries our burdens and has a way of showing us that he never left because He will never leave or forsake us. What an awesome God we serve. He has the ability to keep me while I'm miles away and bring the kind of peace and comfort I need in order to make it through this workday. I felt good about this procedure and the decision to go forward, especially if it will help, in any way, to bring a sense of control to any irregular heart rhythms. The more aids in helping my mom maintain a healthy heart, the better.

I petitioned prayers not only through email but also publicly to coworkers who have also been on this journey with me. I'm so grateful for the kind words of encouragement whether I'm at the coffee pot or the stops on my way to my desk, or if I have a "look" on my face that reveals my unspoken concern after hanging up with my Dad or my sister. I'm not good at covering up how I feel when something is on my mind or bothering me. So just know, I'm not the one to choose for a game of poker. A bad hand is a bad hand and it will be all over my face. Although I love the fact that I'm honest with my expressions, there are times where I wish I could have passed several test when life decided to sucker punch me. Replies to my email came back all day concerning momma and her surgery which really made me feel good. I understand that people do not have to be nice or take your request seriously but they did. These prayers along with my own carried me through a time of day where my focus had to be on my job so of course 5:00pm could not come fast enough.

CHAPTER 9

Wednesday, May 26, 2010

Evans, Charlene

From: Evans, Charlene
Sent: Wednesday, May 26, 2010 2:07 PM
Subject: update on mom 5-26-10

Hello All:

Great news! Fresh off the press! (smile).....Today at 2:30pm, my mom will be leaving the hospital and returning back to Heartland, her physical therapy center, to resume her therapy! Yah Momma! She is so excited and has really been looking forward to working on strengthening her legs to walk again. This is always a good step in the right direction and I'm proud of her. She is so determined to get back to moving and grooving around. She also told me that she will be at my race Oct 30th cheering me on here in Greenville and I believe that she will...how about that for some determination! (SMILE...the thought brings tears of joy to my eyes☺)

Anyway, thanks for your prayers and for encouraging me so...not only through email but even whenever I see you all face to face. It means the world to me and to my mom when I tell her how many people are praying for her!

Blessings!

Charlene

"God is Good!"... say it again, "God IS Good!" Today at 2:30pm my mom was released from the hospital and allowed to resume her physical therapy at Heartland Rehabilitation Center. It's only been a little over 24 hours along with having a three hour surgery that momma is up and moving! I was so excited for her and could hear the excitement in her voice as she prepared to leave the hospital. I knew this was a big deal for my mom because she never liked being in hospitals and her determination for getting well was top on her list. You can't keep a good woman down and this little feisty momma of mine was definitely not the one. She was doing well in therapy before the complications with her heart so I knew after getting this surgery her heart was no longer going to be a hindrance to her progression. The domino effect of health issues took a toll on momma learning how to walk, talk and eat again. I marvel at the fact that a little over seven months ago this incident altered momma's life in a way that no one could fathom. She continues to show us that she is believing God and herself to do the work of healing her body on THIS side of Heaven. Her mental state and having her family around her everyday was her "reason." She persevered through every setback, every set up, every procedure, every surgery because of her will to live. God's plan is never clear but I felt like He was not finished with momma yet. Living through this journey and having front row seats came with an up close and personal encounter with Jesus in a way that altered my focus. The trajectory of my life took a swift turn towards priorities that I easily pushed aside. It gave me the fortitude I needed to revisit dreams, goals, and aspirations as I could hear my mom cheering me on no matter what I had going on at the time. In this current moment it was my first half marathon and I was so excited but nervous. When I made up in my mind that I could do it, the sky was limitless, not only because I believed in myself, but because my momma was already proclaiming her spot right there at the race, cheering me on, and there is no greater feeling in the world than getting her support. I trained ten months for this race and decided to hold off on eating fries and burgers during that time but once the race was done, that would be my victory meal. Along with momma, there were two other ladies that were going through some health challenges who were dear to my heart so I decided to get a t-shirt made to wear for the race. The front of the t-shirt was my "Chiccy Baritone" logo and the back of the shirt said the following,

I am running this half marathon on behalf of:
  1) Viola Evans
  2) Linda Jones
  3) Cameron Jones

I could not wait for my momma to see my shirt as I crossed the finish line! Unfortunately, momma didn't make it to the race because she ended up having dialysis on that day, but as soon as I got home, she was the first phone call I made. Hearing her congratulate me over the phone was an encore of a feeling. I told her about my t-shirt since she was not able to see it for herself and I even showed her a picture once I saw her in person. She just stared at the picture with the biggest smile on her face. Nothing could beat her smile, not even this battle. To still be able to smile while going through what she was going through had to be one of the greatest expressions of courage in the face of adversity. That smile had to endure multiple roadblocks, test and trials. That smile was fighting every fear and hurt internally. That smile, knowing my momma, was not always a real depiction of how she was feeling but she did it anyway because she didn't want us to worry. That smile held stories that were untold for reasons between her and God. The quickest way to not get interrogated was, in some cases, to smile. I can't be mad at her for that because I have found myself doing that—smiling to avoid questions when I didn't want to talk or explain how I REALLY was feeling in that moment because I was still processing something that caused pain. So as she smiled I held off on trying to analyze whether it was authentic and talked about the race since I knew anytime she could remove the focus off of her she welcomed it.

CHAPTER 10

Monday, June 7, 2010

Evans, Charlene

From: Evans, Charlene
Sent: Monday, June 07, 2010 7:55 AM
Subject: update on mom 6-7-10

Good Morning All:

I pray you had a wonderful weekend. Friday my mom was sent back to the hospital due to being nauseous and the nurses can't figure out why. Well, this has been the third incident that she has left the hospital, return back to rehabilitation facility only to be return back to the hospital and we are "ALL" trying to get to the bottom of it. I am thinking maybe the center is preparing her food with something that may not agree with her body...don't know, but will keep you posted as that is being looked on. I went to visit her on Saturday and she is doing a lot better. She was at the hospital but only for dialysis treatment before being returned back to rehabilitation center. She has been so excited about the therapy that she has been receiving and looking forward to walking again soon. Because of her lying in the bed so long and not walking, when she did stand up, her feet were not hitting the ground flat so the doctor suggested that she wears sneakers so that her feet can conform and align themselves up.

Check out the picture of my mom's "All – Stars" or "Chuck Taylors"...LOL!!!

Be blessed,

Charlene

I now have my mom's flower "Chuck Taylors"

Well they say that the 3rd time's a charm right? ***Long sigh*** I can't imagine how my mom must feel right now having to go back to the hospital after only being out for a little over a week. It was frustrating to all of us when we heard it but because my mom exuded so much strength and encouragement, and we all followed suit and focused on what could have been the root to this issue. Since the feeling of being nauseous was under control she still had to get dialysis, so after her treatment she returned back to the rehabilitation center. Whenever there are any medical issues they have to submit the patient to the hospital since the nature of their facility specializes in therapy only. I'm thinking to myself that could be a major inconvenience for someone who is experiencing a life-threatening issue where timing was of the essence. It was also hard to witness her excitement for therapy get interrupted because of this incident. But interruptions are God's way of bringing attention to something in order to change the course of an unfavorable outcome. I used to be so upset and stressed about "interruptions" in my life. I focused more on how it felt debilitating to my motion and unfair to what felt like was progress, but God has allowed me to see with time, age and maturity that interruptions are blessings in disguise. It wasn't that momma was not going to walk again one day because I trusted and believed that it would happen. However, I would always feel for my mom and what she was thinking but not speaking. More than not, her disappointment was never discussed often or at all. She maintained a posture with pain that still amazes me when I think about it. Hindsight into my mom's life through this health scare revealed how consistent she has lived her life when it comes to pain. She found a way to deal with it privately and was careful on what she said and to whom she said it. She understood the power of her words and she only wanted to speak LIFE. It's a phrase I have adopted for myself as it relates to who I am as a woman and for every God given gift. It must speak LIFE and give people a sense of encouragement. I definitely get it from my momma. While going through her therapy she had to get some shoes to help with adjusting her stance and aid in her learning how to walk again so my Dad bought her these flowery chuck taylor sneakers and she fell in love with them. I got so tickled the day I walked in the hospital and noticed them on her feet. She looked so cute and was adjusting to them well. I believe it's the power that comes with having cute shoes. Lying in the hospital bed for so long did a "number" on momma's ability to walk but it didn't stop her. She gained back the strength she needed and it was so inspiring watching her through this process. My mom is such a fighter and her will to live and love was the fuel that kept hope alive and it showed. This soldier would be walking soon and I was anxiously waiting for the day. I know, the bible does say be anxious for nothing . . . but I was anxious because I knew how bad she wanted to walk again and return back to some sort of normalcy with life. That time is coming momma, it's coming.

CHAPTER 11

Wednesday, June 23, 2010

Evans, Charlene

From: Evans, Charlene
Sent: Wednesday, June 23, 2010 8:03 AM
Subject: update on Mom 6-23-10

Hello All!

Just wanted to give you an update on my mom. Friday, June 18th my mom was submitted to the ER because there was blood coming from the defibrillator and it kept bleeding. They removed the device and they also took a blood culture test to make sure her blood was not infected from the device. The test results came back yesterday, June 22nd, and they concluded that the defibrillator was causing an infection so they are working on another alternative for her. She is still in great spirits and still doing very well in physical therapy! June 22nd marked my parents 38th Wedding Anniversary and today, June 23rd marks my birthday! Yah!

Can you say I am BLESSED to see another day, to still have my parents here and to be well in my mind and my body....that is the best birthday gift that I could ever ask for and guess what? It's PRICELESS!

Enjoy your day, continue to keep my mom and family lifted in prayer as we continue to be grateful for the daily prayers and love from our family and friends that has continue to keep us encouraged!

Much Love,

Charlene

… Healing On The Other Side

Today is my 32nd birthday and everyone who knows me knows that birthdays will always be a "big deal" to me. I've been like that all my life and can recall always enjoying my birthday parties growing up as a child. As an adult I did have a surprise birthday party for my 31st birthday, but outside of that birthday, I have not had a birthday "party". This birthday will be one of my most memorable due to my mom's health scare only seven months ago, which was all I was concerned about. I could not imagine being anywhere else but right here at Heartland Rehabilitation Center checking on my girl and of course sharing some laughs with her. That was a GIFT. Being able to look into her eyes and to talk with her. That was a GIFT. Having a conversation with her and sharing updates from my week that included work, traveling, and dating. That was a GIFT. So thank you God for another year of life and to have my momma here for me to still enjoy her company. During this occasion of gratitude I did have to deal with another setback with momma. There was bleeding around her defibrillator that she just had installed through surgery a few weeks ago. After going through some tests to find out what was causing the bleeding they concluded that the device was causing the bleeding and they decided to remove it and seek other alternatives. Even through this setback my momma was in good spirits! I remain amazed at her resilience and her ability to stay positive and keep the faith. I watched my momma and it is true, you learn just as much, or even more, by observing someone, especially when they don't know they are being watched. I have mimicked the way my mom "carried" pain as I think about what I witnessed in her every time I would hear an update of a "setback" about my mom from my sister or my dad. It's not that she was "robotic" or "nonemotional" but she had a calmness in the midst of her current status that confirmed the conversations that she had with God. It was almost as if she would blurt out at any moment, "That's not what God told me," because she didn't falter her disposition. Another blessing outside of my birthday was my parents celebrating their 38th Wedding Anniversary on June 22nd in which my mom has said that it was a possibility that I would have been born on their anniversary but "I waited it out," because I wanted my "own" day of celebrating. Some things I don't care to share and I'm glad that I didn't come on that same day. She believed in love and her marriage, she believed in her children, and told us often and even in the rehabilitation center momma was surrounded by everything that she believed in: Family. I can remember asking my mom what she wanted to be when she was younger and she said I wanted to be a housewife and raise my kids. Nothing brought her more joy. She is the glue that keeps us all together even when we are at odds with each other. She had a way of bringing us all together no matter what and today was no different. Everyone did whatever he or she needed to do to see momma through this therapy. Her cheerleaders were everywhere and there was not a stranger momma met. She connected with everyone she met and it was no mystery that she was the comedian in the family. She kept us in love with what it meant to support family but not without a laugh or two.

CHAPTER

12

Tuesday, July 13, 2010

Healing On The Other Side

Evans, Charlene

From: Evans, Charlene
Sent: Tuesday, July 13, 2010 4:39 PM
Subject: update on my mom 7-13-10

Hello All,

I hope you had a great weekend! I saw my mom on Friday, July 9th and we had a great visit. I was able to see her at the Rehabilitation Center where she is receiving physical therapy every day. She is so excited and ready to leave as soon as her strength is up...and boy is she determined! On Monday, in physical therapy, my sister reported to me that momma took 22 steps on her own! YES, 22 steps! Praise God! My mom has not walked in 7 months and she was so excited! When I saw her on Friday, she told me how she was not trying to get comfortable there because she is ready to go home and she will be walking up to her front door, not getting "wheeled" in...AMEN!!!

While my sister was there, she gave my mom a mini make over coloring her hair and applying some makeup on her face. While she already has beautiful skin, she looked that much more beautiful! Words can not express how proud I am of her and how encouraged she has made me feel about life and the many obstacles...the ups and the downs the in's and out's. Your ATTITUDE is the strongest and most powerful attribute of the human mind and when acknowledged and applied, you can be dangerous! (in a good way of course!!) What a better woman I am because of God being the head of my life, but what an example of strength, courage and resilience I have been awarded because of these traits in my mom... what a time in my life this has been...to watch and pray and witness to the power of healing!

Thank you all for your prayers...please don't stop praying for me and my family!

Much Love,

Charlene

I have been pretty consistent with seeing momma just about every weekend. No matter what is going on, it's always good just to see her. She is back in the rehabilitation center after her therapy was interrupted from her episode of being nauseous and removing the defibrillator since it was causing internal bleeding. That didn't stop momma from pushing herself in therapy in order to walk again. Today I received a call from my sister that my mom took 22 steps on her own! The excitement I felt just hearing that brought tears of joy to me since it has been seven months since my mom has walked. She has maintained an attitude of perseverance and determination through every adversity that she has had to endure in her body and mind. There is nothing too hard for God when He has all of that determination and faith to work with! Wow! What a testimony of her mind, heart, and spirit all being in alignment to want something so bad despite what is going on in. My mom has so many things around her that could have easily discouraged her but she continued to

P.U.S.H. – Pray Until Something Happened.

I could not be any prouder of her in this moment. I had to excuse myself once I finished that phone call and get to a place where I didn't scare my "professional environment," so I went outside my office and walked towards my car as I prayed out loud thanking God with tears running down my face . . . I wanted to run in that parking lot but I feared someone calling security claiming that Charlene lost her mind, so I contain my excitement outside and knew once I got home, I could really get my praise on. This journey has not been easy but my momma has constantly kept a posture of faith through it all. She said she will not be "wheeled" into her home but instead she will be walking up her stairs into her home! I know she was tired being there and desired to be in her home and nothing was going to stop that from happening. Nothing. No illness. No immobility. Nothing.

While this has certainly been a mission for my family I gained so much strength from watching my mom go through this with so much grace. Momma had her eye on the prize and she was sure of her healing. This woman was going to walk again by any means necessary. When I think through the challenges of life growing up and experiencing hurt and pain, I certainly didn't approach them in the way I have witnessed with my mom until I lived a little longer. Like my mom, I have an "old soul" and loved the company of older women ever since I was younger. It didn't change as I got older and what I noticed was I gained so much wisdom from their stories of life. I not only listened with an ear for entertainment but I also listened in order to not repeat it in my own life. Something I have always heard my dad say growing up was, "You will never live long enough to experience every mistake of life and frankly, I don't want to. Listen, learn, and take it for what it is when people share with you mistakes they have made throughout their lives. It's not important to go through it in order to learn from it." That advice became a lot more applicable as I got older because I learned very quickly that bad decisions will cost you something—Time, Money & Regret that you may never recover which could have a profound effect on your future. The cost that I have had to pay for decisions I made growing up are reminders of why I didn't need to experience every bad thing. Some things I am still dealing with but thankfully I have matured through the pain and repercussions of those decisions. I'm so proud of the woman my mom has influenced me to be. The example that this journey has revealed about my mom through one of the most trying times in her life has brought about a change in me. Momma said she was going to walk and she never changed that message. It has been the same ever since she was able to talk again and now she walking again. God is restoring her back and it's simply amazing to witness. Her days at the rehabilitation center are numbered and I'm here for the countdown.

CHAPTER

13

Wednesday, July 28, 2010

Evans, Charlene

From: Evans, Charlene
Sent: Wednesday, July 28, 2010 9:48 AM
Subject: update on my mom 7-28-10

Hello All!

I pray your doing well and this email finds you in good spirits! Wellll............(smiling so hard I can't stand it!).......

There was a family meeting this Monday, July 26th at the Rehabilitation Center with the staff that has been assign to the care and therapy of my mom. The purpose of the meeting was to discuss how far she had progressed and how much longer it will be until she is ready to go home....She has been doing very well and all of her vitals are well, soooo, there is one concern and that is she has an operation that her doctor is going to schedule to remove the feeding tube and her colostomy bag and the downtime and recovery will be closely monitored but outside of that, they project her being ready to go home in

3 WEEKS!!!!!!!!!!!

AHHHHH! I am soo excited and soo proud of her! **8 months and 6 days ago**, no one could foresee where this was going, it was rough on her especially and the family. Through it all we prayed and kept each other encouraged! We reached out to the praying saints and stayed focused on what we need to do in the 'natural' and the 'spiritual' in reference to her full recovery! We spoke LIFE and not DEATH and my momma is coming HOME!

I want to encourage everyone reading this email that **FAITH** and **PATIENCE** are two very hard concepts for anyone regardless of your relationship with Christ. But the reward is so much greater!
P.U.S.H - "Pray Until Something Happens"

Thank you so much for your prayers everyone...it means the world to me and my family! And even though she still has some things to get through she is no where close to where she was and this is so great!

Much Love,

Charlene

Monday of this week there was a meeting at Heartland Rehabilitation Center where momma is receiving her physical therapy. The meeting was scheduled to discuss the timeline of momma's release since she has been doing so well through her therapy. Outside of her upcoming surgery they projected that she will be able to come home in three more weeks!!! *This is a good place to pause and give God PRAISE* I am ecstatic and overjoyed at the news and simply cannot wait to see my mom walk back into the house she made a home. Despite what happened to her eight months and six days ago today, she is determined to get back into the environment that she loves so much so that she can entertain her family and friends in her space. While we are excited about the upcoming release date, there is still one more surgery that momma has to have to remove her feeding tube and colonoscopy bag. Once that is complete, she will be released! WHoooooooooooo Hoooooooooooo! Okay, sorry, I just can't stop smiling because while I see the excitement on her face and witness to her face light up, it ignites everyone else in the room. She has always had that gift—she lights up every room and everyone in it. My momma has a contagious spirit that draws people to her and they don't want to leave her. It also is accompanied by this boisterous laugh that makes me laugh every time I would hear her. Those memories of her talking on the phone early Saturday mornings to her sisters or her girlfriends would be hilarious. I believe the motivation for momma to make sure she got in her phone conversations on a Saturday morning was to wake up early and make sure breakfast was made or that we at least had cereal and milk so that we can fix it ourselves. But I would act like I was watch cartoons but secretly I was trying to catch all of that Saturday morning "tea" momma was spilling. Anytime she would answer the phone she would say funny phrases and proceed with the loudest laugh ever. I was there for it . . .

Every. Saturday. Morning.

Faith and patience are the two words that come to mind when I sum up what this journey has strengthened in me. My faith IN God through all of the uncertainty and miracles that he displayed for me to see weren't by accident. He wanted me to know that faith without work is dead and my mom's constant faith to believe in a different outcome despite how it started was undeniable. She would not have made it out of this situation without her strong faith. But with having faith you must be patient because everything is not instant. We would have never predicted eight months ago that we would still be on this journey eight months later. We had no control of how long it would last so we had to exercise patience. It was not easy but it was worth it. God slowed everyone's life down to focus on what He was taking my mom through in the form of her health, but there was a bigger picture that we all interpreted differently based on where we all were in our individual lives. An interpretation that would change us all forever.

CHAPTER

14

Tuesday, August 17, 2010

Evans, Charlene

From: Evans, Charlene
Sent: Tuesday, August 17, 2010 10:55 AM
Subject: update on my mom 8-17-10

Hello All:

I hope and pray that this email finds everyone in wonderful spirits! Well, Its been a long time coming and for me, this brings me so much joy and emotion. My mom is coming home tomorrow, Wednesday, August 18th and is scheduled for release at 11am. We are soooo excited and ELATED! Words truly can not express what I am feeling right now.

Her desire is to have some time with her immediate family on Wednesday, no visitors or guest, just her children and husband, as she goes through her transition of being HOME again! Then on Saturday, August 21st, we are having a small "Welcome Home" dinner with her siblings and close girlfriends. This indeed is truly a time of celebration for a second chance at LIFE and fulfilling God's purpose in her life! While home she will have "at home" care that will come and monitor for a couple of hours out of the day.

I want to thank my "prayer warriors", my friends and family who have stayed faithful and true to this journey of 8 months...well, go ahead and say 9 months as of Sunday, August 22nd. Your prayers, words of encouragement and faith in the power of prayer and healing restoration is what "kept" us through this very difficult time.

HOW GREAT IS OUR GOD, SING WITH ME, HOW GREEEEEAAAAT IS OUR GOD, AND ALL WILL SEE HOW GREAT, HOW GREAT....IS OUR GOD!!

Much LOVE...signing off for now...

Charlene

I don't believe I can express in words the feeling I felt typing this last email of an almost nine month journey of my mom's health challenges to her walking out of Heartland Rehabilitation Center! Everyone felt relieved and ready for part two of her healing process and getting her back acclimated to being home again. All of my mom's hard work and determination paid off. To witness to her excitement was so special to my family and I. She overcame obstacles that I am still looking at with disbelief. Her language of victory was consistent every step of the way. I will never forget the look in her eyes even in moments where she had the trach and could not speak. It was always a look that spoke to my soul when the fear of the unknown tried to grip me. I watched the same women come in here fighting for her life and now she is leaving alive but still wearing her "invisible" boxing gloves because although she had won several fights, she still had several to go but she wasn't concern or keeping up with how many she had left. She stayed in a positive space of training that kept her in faith. Every time she fell down, she got back up . . . Every time I would see her take a few steps back, she took more steps forward, never dropping her hands but always in the fight. She had so much to fight for and she let us know as often as possible. My warrior is coming home and I could not get to Columbia fast enough from Greenville, SC. Her request and the request of the family were for her to just spend some time with us a few days before allowing any visitors. November 22, 2009 will be a day that none of us will never forget as we feared death but August 18, 2010 God granted my mom a day of rebirth.

These emails reached beyond each recipient as they spoke my mom's name in prayer along with every other person that touched and agreed with them. God appointed prayer warriors from everywhere to agree in unison that Viola C. Evans will live and be healed on this side. His demonstration of this request appeared to be "coming to pass" as we watched God slowly restore my mom's health. Surely what I am witnessing is going to happen and my mom will live through this testimony so that others who are going through or came out will be encouraged and will then encourage others. I can't imagine another outcome because through every prayer and every tear to every hospital and rehabilitation visit up until momma coming home, no one can take the credit for that but God. My mom's faith in God was a partnership in the spirit with Jesus the Christ and God gave us a front row seat. He truly is a Great God and a Powerful God who gives life and allows death. His word proclaims that everyone born will die and while we don't know our "expiration date" we rely a lot on how things appear. But some things will never make sense and the mystery of God in all of His Majesty and Righteousness will never be fully explainable. As I look at my mom sitting in her house, my mind flashbacks to that day and fast forwards quickly to this moment, hoping that my mom doesn't ask me, "What's on your mind?" because I didn't want to lie, but for me I was in awe of God and quickly ran over to my mom hugging her and never wanting her to let me go. As big as I am, my momma still let me jump on her lap and kiss her all over her face as she laughs out loud just like she would on her Saturday morning calls.

Momma is home.

CHAPTER 15

Saturday, April 2, 2011
"My Housewarming"

Healing On The Other Side

Today is my housewarming!!! I bought my first house in Greenville, SC and I'm having a housewarming party hosted by my dear college friend, Latongia Pepper. My guest list included my immediate family, friends from the Greenville area, and my parents. I didn't want a huge gathering but just wanted to include a few people that I was very close to. My housewarming was scheduled from 2:00pm to 5:00pm and for the most part most of my guest had arrived except for my mom and dad. At the time, my parents did not have a GPS (Global Positioning System) but relied on my directions and maps. They apparently were lost getting to my house and throughout the party I was answering calls from them trying to find out where they were and guide them to my house. This was a challenge because I was still new to this area so my guidance was limited. Almost an hour before the party ended my parents finally showed up. I was pleasantly shocked to see my mom because this was also the same day she had her dialysis treatment. Normally after treatment she would be very tired from the four-hour process and would sleep afterwards for about that long, but instead she told my Dad that no matter what she was going to make my housewarming. My Warrior, she truly never ceased to amaze me with all of her might and strength to do what she wanted to do regardless of what was going on. It was good to see my niece, Nymah, who also joined my parents for the special occasion. It felt good for my parents to finally meet some of the people they only knew by name and phone conversations since I've been in Greenville, which was for ten years at this point. I dreamed of owning my first home but knew that I wasn't going to buy immediately when I moved to Greenville, SC from my college town of Orangeburg, SC only because my job included over 75%

traveling. I wanted to wait until I got off the road in order to enjoy having a house. Once I started my next project, which allowed me more time in Greenville, I decided it was time to start the process of buying a house. My mom and dad were so proud of me and it felt so good having them there. My eyes could not escape seeing the gauze over my mom's port with a small spot of blood revealing her recent dialysis treatment as my mind begin analyzing how my mom probably was not feeling her best but she didn't care. She wanted to see her baby's house and I can't deny how giddy I felt inside. I caught her walking around peeking into the rooms on the main floor so I snuck up behind her and followed as she quickly could feel my presence. We locked eyes and she said nothing, but smiled. When we approached the stairs to my second level she hesitated then stopped and turned around. I said, "Momma, you can go upstairs," and she quickly replied, "No baby, I'm good, I know it's nice up there." I knew she was not feeling her best but momma would never say that out loud. She walked around proud and it showed. She made her way to my board for the guest to sign and she left a note that read, "Hey Strawberry Shortcakes, Congrats & Much Love~ Mom & Dad." Momma would call me all kind of food names which was so cute to me ***smile***. It doesn't matter how grown I am, she always talked to me just like I was younger . . . not childish, but definitely in a way that never made me forget that she will always be my mom.

As I was opening my gifts, I surprised my parents with a gift! Ha! I bought them a GPS system and once they realized what it was, along with my guest, we all got a good laugh from the gesture. They were so appreciative of the gift and used it immediately on their way back home. After all my guests left, momma, daddy, and my niece were the last to leave as we all were engaging in conversation about the occasion. My mom was holding my hand as we walked out to the car and she stopped, paused and looked at me. She had a look in her eyes that was so peaceful as she said, **"Your house is beautiful Charlene . . . I'm so proud of you . . . you are in good hands** (referring to my friends in Greenville).**"**

I will never forget those words.

CHAPTER 16

Tuesday, April 26, 2011
"New Beginnings"

Healing On The Other Side

Today was another normal day at work. But will turn out to not be a normal day at all.

I had only been at work for about two hours when I received a phone call from someone I did not recognize. She introduced herself as a neighbor's girlfriend who was a few houses up the street from my parents' house in Columbia. While I got up from my desk and walked over to an area that was away from my coworkers, the lady on the phone began to say to me that I needed to come home and I kept asking her, "Why?" The more we went back and forth, the more I began to feel a strange turn in my stomach. I knew it had something to do with my mom but I did not want to make any suggestions but I didn't want to hear her say what I was thinking. As I was talking to her, I got a call coming in from my brother-in-law, Roni McFarlan, and he said, "Hey baby" and I said, "Hey Roni . . . ," then there was a pause. . . your mother died this morning," and as soon as he said it, I heard my sister in the background crying out. I felt my whole body become numb as I cried out in the office. I lost all consciousness of where I was as several coworkers came to console me and ask what was wrong. From that moment on, my phone began to ring constantly and I just could not bring myself to answer another call because I could not form the words to say through the dagger that just hit my heart.

I had questions. Where is my Dad? Why didn't he call me? Is he OK?

I was in no shape to drive and one of my coworkers drove me home where I threw a few clothes in a bag, grabbed my laptop, and jumped back in the car where I was then driven to Columbia, SC. That drive was a blur as I cried the whole way home. The first thought that came to mind was the phone conversation that I had with my mom the night before she died. She was just released from the hospital that morning after having an episode of acid reflux the night before and she was telling me how she had to sit up in the bed in order to get some sleep because lying down was too painful. I was filling her in on my breakup with a boyfriend I had and she was being her usual self . . . encouraging me and loving on me through the pain and disappointment. She was speaking LIFE into me and telling me that I would get through this. She always knew what to say and like every phone call coming to an end, momma never hung up without saying, "I Love You," but I didn't have a clue at all that she was not feeling well but I'm so grateful that my last conversation with my mom would be one that I will cherish forever.

"God, I thought you were going to heal my mom on THIS side?"

God answered back and said, "I never promised you that."

But in my spirit, that answer wasn't good enough. At first I started to "fuss" at God the way Job did and God referred me back to his response to Job in the bible in Job Chapter 38 – 42.

The Lord Speaks Job 38-42 (NIV)

Job 38:

¹Then the Lord spoke to Job out of the storm. He said: ²"Who is this that obscures my plans with words without knowledge? ³Brace yourself like a man; I will question you, and you shall answer me. ⁴"Where were you when I laid the earth's foundation? Tell me, if you understand. ⁵Who marked off its dimensions? Surely you know! Who stretched a measuring line across it? ⁶On what were its footings set, or who laid its cornerstone - ⁷while the morning stars sang together and all the angels shouted for joy? ⁸"Who shut up the sea behind doors when it burst forth from the womb, ⁹when I made the clouds its garment and wrapped it in thick darkness, ¹⁰when I fixed limits for it and set its doors and bars in place, ¹¹when I said, 'This far you may come and no farther; here is where your proud waves halt'? ¹²"Have you ever given orders to the morning, or shown the dawn its place, ¹³that it might take the earth by the edges and shake the wicked out of it? ¹⁴The earth takes shape like clay under a seal; its features stand out like those of a garment. ¹⁵The wicked are denied their light, and their upraised arm is broken. ¹⁶"Have you journeyed to the springs of the sea or walked in the recesses of the deep? ¹⁷Have the gates of death been shown to you? Have you seen the gates of the deepest darkness? ¹⁸Have you comprehended the vast expanses of the earth? Tell me, if you know all this. ¹⁹"What is the way to the abode of light? And where does darkness reside? ²⁰Can you take them to their places? Do you know the paths to their dwellings? ²¹Surely you know, for you were already born! You have lived so many years! ²²"Have you entered the storehouses of the snow or seen the storehouses of the hail, ²³which I reserve for times of trouble, for days of war and battle? ²⁴What is the way to the place where the lightning is

dispersed, or the place where the east winds are scattered over the earth? ²⁵Who cuts a channel for the torrents of rain, and a path for the thunderstorm, ²⁶to water a land where no one lives, an uninhabited desert, ²⁷to satisfy a desolate wasteland and make it sprout with grass? ²⁸Does the rain have a father? Who fathers the drops of dew? ²⁹From whose womb comes the ice? Who gives birth to the frost from the heavens ³⁰when the waters become hard as stone, when the surface of the deep is frozen? ³¹"Can you bind the chains of the Pleiades? Can you loosen Orion's belt? ³²Can you bring forth the constellations in their seasons or lead out the Bear with its cubs? ³³Do you know the laws of the heavens? Can you set up God's dominion over the earth? ³⁴"Can you raise your voice to the clouds and cover yourself with a flood of water? ³⁵Do you send the lightning bolts on their way? Do they report to you, 'Here we are'? ³⁶Who gives the ibis wisdom or gives the rooster understanding? ³⁷Who has the wisdom to count the clouds? Who can tip over the water jars of the heavens ³⁸when the dust becomes hard and the clods of earth stick together? ³⁹"Do you hunt the prey for the lioness and satisfy the hunger of the lions ⁴⁰when they crouch in their dens or lie in wait in a thicket? ⁴¹Who provides food for the raven when its young cry out to God and wander about for lack of food?

Job 39:

¹"Do you know when the mountain goats give birth? Do you watch when the doe bears her fawn? ²Do you count the months till they bear? Do you know the time they give birth? ³They crouch down and bring forth their young; their labor pains are ended. ⁴Their young thrive and grow strong in the wilds; they leave and do not return. ⁵"Who let the wild donkey go free? Who untied its ropes? ⁶I gave it the wasteland as its home, the salt flats

as its habitat. ⁷It laughs at the commotion in the town; it does not hear a driver's shout. ⁸It ranges the hills for its pasture and searches for any green thing. ⁹"Will the wild ox consent to serve you? Will it stay by your manger at night? ¹⁰Can you hold it to the furrow with a harness? Will it till the valleys behind you? ¹¹Will you rely on it for its great strength? Will you leave your heavy work to it? ¹²Can you trust it to haul in your grain and bring it to your threshing floor? ¹³"The wings of the ostrich flap joyfully, though they cannot compare with the wings and feathers of the stork. ¹⁴She lays her eggs on the ground and lets them warm in the sand, ¹⁵unmindful that a foot may crush them, that some wild animal may trample them. ¹⁶She treats her young harshly, as if they were not hers; she cares not that her labor was in vain, ¹⁷for God did not endow her with wisdom or give her a share of good sense. ¹⁸Yet when she spreads her feathers to run, she laughs at horse and rider. ¹⁹"Do you give the horse its strength or clothe its neck with a flowing mane? ²⁰Do you make it leap like a locust, striking terror with its proud snorting? ²¹It paws fiercely, rejoicing in its strength, and charges into the fray. ²²It laughs at fear, afraid of nothing; it does not shy away from the sword. ²³The quiver rattles against its side, along with the flashing spear and lance. ²⁴In frenzied excitement it eats up the ground; it cannot stand still when the trumpet sounds. ²⁵At the blast of the trumpet it snorts, 'Aha!' It catches the scent of battle from afar, the shout of commanders and the battle cry. ²⁶"Does the hawk take flight by your wisdom and spread its wings toward the south? ²⁷Does the eagle soar at your command and build its nest on high? ²⁸It dwells on a cliff and stays there at night; a rocky crag is its stronghold. ²⁹From there it looks for food; its eyes detect it from afar. ³⁰Its young ones feast on blood, and where the slain are, there it is."

Job 40:

¹The Lord said to Job: ²"Will the one who contends with the Almighty correct him? Let him who accuses God answer him!" ³Then Job answered the Lord: ⁴"I am unworthy—how can I reply to you? I put my hand over my mouth. ⁵I spoke once, but I have no answer - twice, but I will say no more." ⁶Then the Lord spoke to Job out of the storm: ⁷"Brace yourself like a man; I will question you, and you shall answer me. ⁸"Would you discredit my justice? Would you condemn me to justify yourself? ⁹Do you have an arm like God's, and can your voice thunder like his? ¹⁰Then adorn yourself with glory and splendor, and clothe yourself in honor and majesty. ¹¹Unleash the fury of your wrath, look at all who are proud and bring them low, ¹²look at all who are proud and humble them, crush the wicked where they stand. ¹³Bury them all in the dust together; shroud their faces in the grave. ¹⁴Then I myself will admit to you that your own right hand can save you. ¹⁵"Look at Behemoth, which I made along with you and which feeds on grass like an ox. ¹⁶What strength it has in its loins, what power in the muscles of its belly! ¹⁷Its tail sways like a cedar; the sinews of its thighs are close-knit. ¹⁸Its bones are tubes of bronze, its limbs like rods of iron. ¹⁹It ranks first among the works of God, yet its Maker can approach it with his sword. ²⁰The hills bring it their produce, and all the wild animals play nearby. ²¹Under the lotus plants it lies, hidden among the reeds in the marsh. ²²The lotuses conceal it in their shadow; the poplars by the stream surround it. ²³A raging river does not alarm it; it is secure, though the Jordan should surge against its mouth. ²⁴Can anyone capture it by the eyes, or trap it and pierce its nose?

Job 41:

¹"Can you pull in Leviathan with a fishhook or tie down its tongue with a rope? ²Can you put a cord through its nose or pierce its jaw with a hook? ³Will it keep begging you for mercy? Will it speak to you with gentle words? ⁴Will it make an agreement with you for you to take it as your slave for life? ⁵Can you make a pet of it like a bird or put it on a leash for the young women in your house? ⁶Will traders barter for it? Will they divide it up among the merchants? ⁷Can you fill its hide with harpoons or its head with fishing spears? ⁸If you lay a hand on it, you will remember the struggle and never do it again! ⁹Any hope of subduing it is false; the mere sight of it is overpowering. ¹⁰No one is fierce enough to rouse it. Who then is able to stand against me? ¹¹Who has a claim against me that I must pay? Everything under heaven belongs to me. ¹²"I will not fail to speak of Leviathan's limbs, its strength and its graceful form. ¹³Who can strip off its outer coat? Who can penetrate its double coat of armor? ¹⁴Who dares open the doors of its mouth, ringed about with fearsome teeth? ¹⁵Its back has rows of shields tightly sealed together; ¹⁶each is so close to the next that no air can pass between. ¹⁷They are joined fast to one another; they cling together and cannot be parted. ¹⁸Its snorting throws out flashes of light; its eyes are like the rays of dawn. ¹⁹Flames stream from its mouth; sparks of fire shoot out. ²⁰Smoke pours from its nostrils as from a boiling pot over burning reeds. ²¹Its breath sets coals ablaze, and flames dart from its mouth. ²²Strength resides in its neck; dismay goes before it. ²³The folds of its flesh are tightly joined; they are firm and immovable. ²⁴Its chest is hard as rock, hard as a lower millstone. ²⁵When it rises up, the mighty are terrified; they retreat before its thrashing. ²⁶The sword that reaches it has no effect, nor does the spear or the dart or the javelin. ²⁷Iron it treats like straw and bronze like rotten wood. ²⁸Arrows do not make it

flee; slingstones are like chaff to it. ²⁹A club seems to it but a piece of straw; it laughs at the rattling of the lance. ³⁰Its undersides are jagged potsherds, leaving a trail in the mud like a threshing sledge. ³¹It makes the depths churn like a boiling caldron and stirs up the sea like a pot of ointment. ³²It leaves a glistening wake behind it; one would think the deep had white hair. ³³Nothing on earth is its equal - a creature without fear. ³⁴It looks down on all that are haughty; it is king over all that are proud."

Job 42:

¹Then Job replied to the Lord: ²"I know that you can do all things; no purpose of yours can be thwarted. ³You asked, 'Who is this that obscures my plans without knowledge?' Surely I spoke of things I did not understand, things too wonderful for me to know. ⁴"You said, 'Listen now, and I will speak; I will question you, and you shall answer me.' ⁵My ears had heard of you but now my eyes have seen you. ⁶Therefore I despise myself and repent in dust and ashes."

As I read those chapters I could relate to how angry Job was but to hear God's rebuttal was humbling, to say the least. During this time of anguish, I said the following to God:

> "I saw you perform miracles on this journey that were clear that her end was not near. She went from a normal life of talking, walking and eating to not talking, walking and eating and learning how to talk, walk and eat again in a 9 month period! How amazing to witness to the power of prayer and faith join together to produce results. That didn't have to happen and she could have died at a point where she was already in ICU and it would have made more sense to me. But you allowed me to see you bring my mom out of this period of affliction, restore her health to a point of normalcy and now she is dead. My mind wants to understand your plan. My heart just wants my mom back on earth again. But my spirit… It astonishes me outside of my mind and my heart. It follows YOU and creates a peace that surpasses my understanding that has not only brought comfort through pain but also a confirmation that this is YOUR plan. It rejoiced in her transition from life to death. My solace in the aftermath of her passing is grounded in my faith in YOU, my Lord and Savior Jesus The Christ and not undermining YOUR sovereignty because YOU can do all things. This was not a mistake, it was ordained and already known from the time she was born. "A person's days are determined; you (God) have decreed the number of his months and have set limits he cannot exceed." -Job 14:5 (NIV)."

Because I love God and I believe in His word, it doesn't mean that my humanity would automatically respond in the way my spirit did in that moment. My mind reminds me of my mom constantly. Every day. Her, my father, Quanita and DeWayne are the only ones that have known me all my life and that's not a bond that is broken in any number of years under any circumstance. The gratitude in the timing of my mom's death is the fact that I had 33 years lived and loved with her and her influence on my life continues. Her spirit is mimicked in family members and strangers. I will never forget taking my first trip out of the country to Mumbai, India the first year that she died. I had a layover in Amsterdam and that flight had over 200 people with most of the passengers being of Indian descent, except for one lady who was an African American woman, and I thought to myself when I saw her in the security line prior to boarding the plane, "I wonder where she is going in India?"

I was soon going to find out because guess who was sitting right next to her? ME!

How could this be possible? This was crazy in such a wonderful way because she talked to me the whole trip. She was around my mom's age and shared with me her trip details and since learning that I was traveling internationally for the first time, she began to give me advice about being in India and when we landed in India she took my hand and guided me through filling out the entry forms and showed me how to get through customs. She gave me a quick lesson on exchanging my money and before she left to go her separate way, she gave me her phone number and told me to call her if I needed anything while being abroad and also once I returned back to the states. That experience left me in awe of God and all I could think to myself was, "She truly has the spirit of my

MOM and like my mom, she wanted to make sure I was ok knowing that I had moments of fear all because the experience was unknown to me and I was so far away from home." When I returned to the states I tried calling that number and it just keep ringing, never going to voicemail. I tried several more times and the same response every time. I wonder if she was angel?

My new normal is far from feeling normal as the absence of my mom has altered my view of life. This cycle of Life and Death continues to shed more and more family and friends as I hold on as tight as I can to memories, lessons, blessings shared. I can't say that I have mastered the concept of living everyday as if it is my last, but there are moments in every day where I say to myself what if today IS my last day? Have I pursued every assignment on my life that God has placed in my heart? Have I repented for things known and unknown that I may have said or done? Have I prayed for forgiveness for people I may have hurt? Did I truly accept forgiveness from people who have hurt me? Did I operate in obedience when God spoke to my heart and told me to call someone, pray for someone, bless someone, or simply smile at someone who at the time needed it more than I would have ever know? I have fashioned my life behind not only hearing the word and desiring to please God in what He tells me to do but also being a "doer" of the word.

> [22]*Do not merely listen to the word, and so deceive yourselves. Do what it says.* [23]*Anyone who listens to the word but does not do what it says is like someone who looks at his face in a mirror* [24]*and, after looking at himself, goes away and immediately forgets what he looks like.* [25]*But whoever looks intently into the*

perfect law that gives freedom, and continues in it—not forgetting what they have heard, but doing it—they will be blessed in what they do. -James 1:22-25 (NIV)

I rejoice in not assuming, or hoping, but knowing that my mom is in no more pain, publicly or privately. She has completed the race of life and has left me with 33 years of lessons that I pray I will be able to use whether it helps me or someone else. My desire is to give the kind of unconditional love that I have received from my mom and my God to every person I encounter, and if I get a laugh out of the deal the way my mom had the ability to do, well, that will be a bonus.

R.I.S.P. ~ Rest In Sweet Peace
Viola Corrine Evans
2/11/52 – 4/26/11

P.S: Your Legacy Lives On . . .

ABOUT THE AUTHOR

Charlene Evans, introduced to the poetry circuit in 2001 and affectionately named, "Chiccy Baritone" (Pronounced "chick-y") has used her deep melodic voice to speak LIFE through Poetry, Public Speaking, Workshops and Conferences nationally and internationally.

Born and raised in Columbia, SC, Charlene Evans attended South Carolina State University and obtained her degree in Electrical Engineering Technology. Following graduation she moved to Greenville, SC in 2001 where she worked professionally in various fields that includes: Electrical Engineering, Project Controls and Product Development. While still working professionally, in 2007, Chiccy Baritone has always had a heart for philanthropy, so she started a poetry showcase called, "R U Skooled? From A Woman's Perspective Poetically," raising money through sponsorship and community giving for a local nonprofit of choice. The night of the show, she presents the donations to the selected nonprofit on stage after various performances from local and national acclaimed female Poets.

While R U Skooled? From A Woman's Perspective Poetically was still going on, in 2012, Chiccy Baritone launched Breakfast For Champions Women Empowering Women Sessions, which taught women the importance of networking and igniting their God given purpose. These sessions ranged over a 3-month period for

5 years and covered various topics with expertise from local and national speakers, personal development exercises, and nontraditional networking dialogue among women who ranged between the ages of 25 to 50. These sessions produced new business ideas, business owners, authors, friendships, mentors, and so much more, but most importantly, various tools and resources needed to move forward in destiny.

In December 2017, Chiccy Baritone relocated to Atlanta, GA by faith after living in Greenville, SC for 16 years. Within a year of relocating she launched her new business, Chiccy Baritone Unlimited, LLC, and was featured in VoyageATL Magazine, she Joined the Toastmasters District 14 Midtown Club called, "The Stammering Churchills," and continues to use her voice around the world for

"Self Expression | World Outreach | People Progression."

Her recognition includes: Being a TEDxGreenville performer, which is part of the prestigious nationally and internationally recognized TED (Technology, Entertainment and Design) conference, a writer for several projects with Billy Graham Evangelistic Association, which included voiceover work, monthly devotionals, and videos featuring her original poems, "LIPS: Proverbs 18:21 and GAP for "Rock The River" tour, feature U.S poet at The University of Pretoria in Pretoria, South Africa for their "UnMasked" poetry event, Greenville Magazine, "Young, Gifted and Black -16 African Americans changing the face of Greenville," South Carolina State University (SCSU) Review Magazine, "Distinguish Alumni under 40," IMARA Woman Magazine cover and feature article, The G Magazine of Greenville, "Saved By The Written Word" feature, Talk Greenville Magazine article "Extreme Hobbies," Greenville Newspaper Lifestyle Section Feature Article, "Women of Success" Award Recipient, "Ignite The Mic" competition winner for Poetry Category along with numerous television, radio, national poetry and keynote speaking engagements.

To learn more about CHICCY BARITONE visit:
Website: www.chiccybaritone.com

Made in the USA
Columbia, SC
19 June 2019